Surya Harry is an author and poet. She had been taken into writing since 2004. *Stream of Thought* is a collection of her favourites. Surya's work has previously been published in a poetry anthology and an online magazine. Poetry is personal; it can be uplifting, tragic, peaceful, imaginative, sad, or hilarious. Whatever it emotes is to be experienced. She went to the University of Kerala to pursue her love of introspection and words, receiving her Bachelor of Arts in English. She grew up in Trivandrum, Kerala, before moving to Dubai, the place she calls her second home, where she indulges in various creative activities. Surya is a human resources professional but a writer and dancer at heart.

In loving memory of my parents,
To my husband Joseph and my son Peter,
My family, my ever-inspiring friends.

Surya Harry

STREAM OF THOUGHT

Memories of Mindspace

AUSTIN MACAULEY PUBLISHERS™

LONDON • CAMBRIDGE • NEW YORK • SHARJAH

ISBN – 9789948756156 – (Paperback)
ISBN – 9789948756163 – (E-Book)

Application Number: MC-10-01-0712423
Age Classification: E

The age group that matches the content of the books has been classified according to the age classification system issued by the UAE Media Council.

First Published 2024
AUSTIN MACAULEY PUBLISHERS FZE
Sharjah Publishing City
P.O Box [519201]
Sharjah, UAE
www.austinmacauley.ae
+971 655 95 202

Prologue

Love you Amma

In her debut poetry collection, Surya (my Amma) invites readers into a world where every verse is a delicate flavor waiting to be savored. Whether you choose to indulge in a few pieces at a time or immerse yourself fully, each page promises a profound experience. This collection is a gift for book lovers of all stripes, offering a blend of modern poetry and timeless epics that soothes the spirit. With voices spanning the globe, she has managed to navigate the depths of human emotion, from grief and rage to joy and love. With every turn of its pages offering a new insight with each reading, this is a book to revisit.

Peter Joseph

Month of December

Wintry morning, ground draped in white
Sing a song of snowy nights, winds cold and dreary
Sitting here by the embers, each heart is happy
Missing people our hearts still hold on
Joyful thoughts flood my mind, of seasons gone by,
Grand old December, we welcome you once more,
Mom, you are missed so deeply, hear no loving voice;
Each year roll around, I am further in this pain steeply.
Memories come flooding back to me of you,
Celebrations you lovingly prepared, thoughts good and bad,
Livingroom scented of evergreen memories of yester years,
With family and friends and lots of cheer,
To my heart, without my wish, comes my cries and loneliness,
December, you're never easy, but I always leave you happier.

Down the Hills

So we begin, wind in the hair
To the queen of hill stations
Tall shimmering silver oaks pair
Blue and cream wooden coaches.

With large open windows,
Majestically, chugs and muffles.
Through charming Nilgiris Hill
Hauled up hill, a torrent of water spill.

Columns of smokes blue and cream,
Pass the babbling brooks, tether
The starry sky sparked a fire in me
Lot to recollect in such pacific weather.

The air here is tea fragrant.
Women pluck two leaves and a bud.
Toss them into baby basket.
Trundling through the tea, mud.

Sneaking through a hole in the rock,
Blind turn, to delightful backdrops viewable!
"Her Majesty" up the tea garden, picture block.
A marvel, the teeth, that holds the train moveable.

Chimney

Of all the festival, Christmas awakens,
The strongest, heartfelt memories.
A tone of solemn and sacred feeling,
Lifts the spirits to an elevated enjoying.

Christmas is a holiday for friends
A grander effect of music on feelings
A time of joy, to think of those we love,
Season of enjoyment, families far and wide.

In restless struggle of life,
Reunited, meet once again.
A happy state of companionship.
Old recollections, dormant sympathies.

Christmas time awakens!
Hopes, St. Nick, would be there
In a small sleigh, and eight reindeer
Down the chimney!

A bundle of toys on his back
His eyes, how they twinkled!
His dimples, how merry!
His cheeks like a cherry!

His mouth drawn up like a bow!
Bead on the chin, as white as snow!
A pipe held tight in his teeth,
Smoke encircles his head, like a wreath!

Round belly shook like a jelly, when he laughed!
Filled all the stockings, sprang to his sleigh.
Flew like down a thistle. Drove out of sight.
Singing Merry Christmas!

Waiting

I hold my hands and wait,
I wait with joy the coming year
My heart shall reap where it hath sown
And garner up its fruit of tears.

We are here on planet earth.
Things move at the speed of light.
There is no slow and waiting.
It was just right for those like us.

Waiting for food, services and men,
We even wait nine months for birth.
Waiting for red lights to turn green,
Here we are now waiting again.

Joy and sadness fill my days.
My heart and soul are aching,
I long to see you soon again
To end the eternal waiting.

I have been waiting night and day
I didn't see the time,
I waited all through my life
I am waiting for the miracle to come.

Yes, another year is over
"Children" still not home,
My heart is so heavy
I feel so alone "waiting".

Emptiness

In a home distant, far away
Sat an old woman.
The withered face like,
An autumn leaf dry and fragile.

Her hand shook, transparent skin,
Yellowed nails, with grey hair.
Each age wrapped around her like
Another layer of onion skin.

She remembers her wedding day,
But not what she had for lunch.
Judge me not, not like a judge
For there is more of me to see.

Although when you look at me,
This is what you see.
Old age, an awful isolation,
Without children to be with.

New Beginning

I stand here wondering what to say.
In an emotional roller coaster
Of yes and no, okay and may be
And then, all of a sudden,

I began to think of beginning,
A glorious sunrise in the East
A new day, a new beginning.
Yesterdays are left behind.

Present and future will to me be very kind.
A path way unknown to me.
Sometimes I walk alone
Sometimes other footsteps join me.

Best beginnings sometimes end in sorrow.
But I smell the spring in the winter chill.
Even on our darkest days.
The sun shines tomorrow.

New beginning, fresh as morning dew.
Our chance to start anew, the beginning now.
Dreams can come true,
That's the wonder of a rainbow.

Loveliness

Beauty is like fog encircling everything
The hands awake you, insinuating you to write
The best treasure of one's eye;
It is in the heart which touches another.

Beauty is unexplainable, everywhere at everyplace,
There is more that you can't see.
The eagle glides with grandiose wings,
Close to the sun in lonely lands.

Flying over wonderful mountains
Beneath him the wrinkled sea crawls.
The sun is sinking, illuminating the sky
The serenity of evening brings peace to my soul.

I feel a sweet soft breeze across my face.
The shadows of trees are now silhouetted;
There are no noises to be heard,
The evening is one of pure serenity.

Moon so full and bright breathes the place in its silver light,
I stood as mute witness to this beauty around.
Immerse myself in your serene blanket.
Oh, how lucky I am! To save this experience.

Overflow

Shower tumbles on the stretches for days
Thrashing and crushing the ground futile
Sinking her regularly, as she come up for air.

This is a felony on my city.
Pitter-patter on the earth suddenly,
They quicken into a roaring song.

A threatening chant, the rumble
of a liquid being, whose shape,
not one you can contain.

Giant loads of water, mighty life-giving force.
Doomed murderer, too much for us to take.
Faith tested, beyond our reach.

God's land drowning in tears!
We braced in the refuges and prayed for relief.
A massive hard rain falling on our home.

Casing our memories, drowning our hopes
Washing away the lives and homes we made
The sounds of tragedy still linger behind.

In the darkness, we found heroes,
Rising from this drenched hell,
Helping neighbours, if shelter.
Opening their doors to strangers
Soon the sun will rise high,
Above the crystal-clear blue skies.

To be reminded of a special place,
Filled with promise, ranged with strength
It is a place so few will realise.

Meeting with Love

The first time we spoke;
He looked right into my eyes,
Never dropped his gaze.
Much to surprise
His smile was so cute
Laughter so absolute
Words were like magic
Eyes were what enchanted me.

The wondrous moment of our meeting…
I well remember you appear
Tender voice kept sounding,
As worldly bustle to my ear.
I never thought I ever learn to love,
Yet I found myself so in love with you.
You were sent from above,
To be my one true love.

His interest seemed real,
And the time we spent was great
You finally whispered in my ear;
Three little words I longed to hear.
Now years later I turned back,
The Sun behind me, nothing has changed
I have not permitted any change.
I am going to keep things same.

Innocence

The day was calm along
A dreamy river flowing
I paddle my way home
Follows the river as it bends,
I know nothing about, boat and the river.

The boat is moving slowly
I am feeling inside myself,
All the happiness and peace
Innocence is rarer than ever;
Shall I compare thee to the purest white?

Or truth, only few speak
Peace to my soul to bring
Often called the dove, thy father
Thy mother often accompanies,
Her heavenly Father.

The meekest of His Creation, Lamb.
Thy sisters, swans of goodly hue
Children thy friends! Simple and care free
Eyes so clear, without any doubt.
Innocent like a rainbow.

Rainy afternoon, fresh as morning dew
We see it in the eyes of young, believe it in a world
Bent on craze and confusion, it protects us!
Even when we think it is gone,
A part remains inside us?

Realisation

I began an inner journey with my precious life,
Taking inner and inner, where I feel belief,
Started unravelling each of my masks
They are ten and thousands in numbers.

All human faces fit them, here or there
A school boy, financier, or a ruler,
Professional mask and family mask,
Friends mask or the acquaintance mask.

A different mask for next door.
Depending on the nature
We have a mask to cover the face.
A mask that grins and lies.

Hides our cheeks and shades our eyes.
I'll wear the mask and I'm afraid I drive
I wear them to hide, what I sense;
I'll be shot down and walked everywhere.

Or let down and stepped on.
I wear the mask to hide rejection and confliction.
My mask conceals thousand feelings;
I am scared to take off my masks.

Beneath lays my fear, weakness, confusion, and loneliness.
Are those true versions of myself beyond silliness;
Never let myself sink, time for me is today,
To do things in my own way.

Love, a Solemn Music

On a Summer Sunday evening
We walked forth to view the waning
Sky turns ruby as sun prepares for his snooze.
Hand in hand we walk through the shore.

Through the water's edge for a quick splash of cool ocean.
And to spent some quite moments.
The sand feels rusty and thin, filling the gaps of our toes.
Never ceasing waves play across the shores.

Waves hum calm ears; your arms envelop me.
Head resting over your shoulder, softly speak your name.
I try to memorise you; way you walked, looked back;
Over your shoulder, I felt everything right.

You kiss me sweet and softly, sensed your warm gentle touch,
Helped me feel protected, under the stary sky.
Nowhere else I want to be, hand in hand, you, and me!
Cherish the thought, a forever, knows no boundaries.

Dressed in Robe White

The snow queen walked slowly in the midnight,
So cold was her smile and hand, eyes blue,
Snowflakes fluttered over the house tops and street,
Delicate, untouched, and pure, is found the ground below.
Branches on the evergreen dressed in snowy white,
Wake up to a world of white, blanket from another,
Nothing to be seen for miles, but my footsteps,
No one has been here, first one to explore
Outside is cold, everyone is freezing.
No place to go, fireside is delightful.
Children come and play,
some roll it to make balls and others the snowman,
Snow queen left, with dawn's weak early light,
Behind her was silence and white.

Anxiety

I am endlessly dazed, heart won't slow down
The feeling creeps for every dark place.
It's melting me from inside, fills up my head
Invading my space, weakening the bones.

The fire inside, it's my anxiety.
Feeling like I'm in a fish bowl.
Kind of fear, long lasting
Like a sweater wore my fretfulness.

Everywhere you followed me,
Watching me claw at my inside
You are my master and I am your slave
Giggle in my dreams, haunt my life and alter my thoughts.

Taunting me, you take my joy and you can't be seen.
You are not my friend nor enemy
Though you made me strong, not your prisoner,
I left you at the door, don't need you anymore.

Fairy with a Rolling Pin

Every day I stand before the kitchen island,
I begin again from the scratch,
I measured out flour and water,
And yes, ghee and a pinch of salt.

Knead constantly and liberally and fold,
Then thought – take a quick nap
On to the couch and drew up a blanket.
I drifted off quickly and knew not how long?

I was woken by the clang of a pot,
So, I got to my feet, quite fixed to spy.
Peering inside the kitchen – I saw
Not a cat or mice as I thought.

But a fairy making roti,
Punching down the risen dough,
To shape the loaf with care,
Rolling carefully using a rolling pin,
On the well-floured board.

Now in the pan and turn after minutes,
Brush with extra spoon of love (ghee),
The house is smelling great.
My fairy washed all the dishes and put them away.

Cleaned my house – spotless!
As she turned once,
Gave a quick wink and gone,
And she was my mamma's daughter!

Lovely Little Angel

A dear little face, I like so to kiss,
Has such a sunny smile, hold, oh so close,
Don't ever let them go, shown from heaven above
Hold and rock, kiss good night, wrap my arms around.

Those little arms hold me tight, find me in the night,
So as to feel everything is exact, little kisses sweep on my face,
Tiny arms wrap me in embrace, little smile on cute face for me,
Sticky fingers, tangled hair, scattered crayons everywhere.

Fancy creation on the wall, scraped-up hands from falling.
Endless hugs and goofy wet kisses, all in the life of a precious
child,
My little one how I adore you! so innocent, pure, and true,
Child you will grow up soon, be cheerful and mild,
Must not be fretful and cry!

Speechless Flight

Death is nothing new, that sometime in a sigh;
The eloquent breath shall take its speechless flight.
It comes with light speed and without a clue,
And all life's ruddy springs forget to flow.

To some it come quickly and painless,
To others it comes with soreness.
Death has always been around.
The impact is just like weather.

You never knew how it's going to be;
Next time it may strike you or me.
Taught me how to cherish,
Those whom I hold so dear.

Showed me not to take life granted,
And to show others how much I care.
No one wants to talk about death;
Some try to avoid, some silent.

But as sure as we are born; we die;
Resurrect in the minds of whom we love.
It broke our hearts to lose you, but you did not go alone,
For part of us went with you on the day He called you home.

College Days

Everything is fresh in my mind,
Wish life could just rewind,
Let's laugh, play, and rejoice,
Once again become a college girl.

Thoughts of class mates returned,
After few years, with tears of pangs
Everyone now busy, as none,
Has escaped the destiny's plot.

Notes reviewed to literary musings,
Handles to last bench games,
Cultural rehearsals, to club inaugurations,'
Superiors watched all with hawk-like eyes.

Each year our college have, the inter college dance;
The only time we would have other gender in campus,
Dance was Monday noon, boys smoke along the way,
She sprung before them, frog-marched them!

The night before finals, all through the college,
All in hands folded for last minute knowledge,
In my own home, I had been pacing,
Dreading exams, I soon would be facing.

Most were quite sleepy, but I couldn't touch the bed,
Visions of essays danced in heads, I drained all the coffee,
I stared at my notes, but my thoughts were muddy,
My eyes went blur; I just couldn't study.

I nearly concluded that life was too cruel,
With futures depending on grades had in college,
Just did my best, happy finals to all,
And to all, a good test.

Chatting and laughing, we all were in elation,
Till the moments of separation,
When it was time to part,
We returned with a heavy heart.

Today life is full of commitments,
And too many worries,
But those cherished moments,
Will live forever in our memories.

Truth

Light went looking for truth with bright eyes
Hoping to shine upon lies;
Whatever darkness it wore for hiding
Wide and unblinking concentration never stirred
Light was in for the search of its life
There was more darkness than light.

I step out of the dark and into the light;
There I see the beauty of life
Love, harmony, peace, compassion;
Truth, honesty, faithfully loyal companions
I see the beauty of humanity, honest fear, painful secrets,
Deceptive truth to be true to one's self.

Darkness had permits to go places light cannot follow
For darkness is older than light, is always everywhere light is
not,
The moment light arrived darkness would escape undetected
A truth not to be ignored but acknowledged
Bringing us into the grey middle
Where we can see the truth and beauty in all.
Temptation, infatuation, copulation, lust
These are the tempting earthly rewards,
Short termed and deadly up from the dust,
Revelation, adoration, inspiration, love,
These are the things that reside in us,
Floating from the wings of dove.

Thoughtful, compassion, mercy, life,
These are the pearls sent from above
So, we can overcome all the strife,
Tribulation, restitution, institution, loss,
These are the bonds that divide us all up,
Chained to our ankles, all cluttered and rough.

Truth is our weapon to fight against sin
A young child's smile or magpie's call,
Is what you think, perceive, and feel,
Unconditional share of being,
Truth is what you make of it;
Let us stand in TRUTH.

Painting the Sky

The clouds are blowing in,
Sun slowly disappears;
Or is he playing hide and seek?
The white shape silhouetted
Against a blue background
My favourite things;
Like to stare at clouds.

It changes every page,
It is cotton cuddly,
Cute and soft,
Puffy and dark,
Swiftly in the sky,
Those cumulus clouds,
Are no sign of rain,
But fair weather!

They come in shapes,
Is it a rabbit, a dragon, or an angel?
Clouds are special for people and Sun,
Lots of different type,
Black, grey, and white,
Some fluffy and some flat,
Blocks the shiny Sun.
Birds and planes fly through them,
I like the cumulonimbus clouds.

Fighting Fear

I imagine this midnight;
My eyes closed,
Is something else alive?
Beside the clock's loneliness.

Something more nearby,
Though deeper within darkness;
Is entering fear…
I have never done it again.

Fear engulfing my dark hole of the head,
This illness, I have suffered for so long.
I wish I could get over it,
And it hurts when people pick.

I wish I could stay strong,
I am telling myself not to fear,
Telling myself not to cry is hard to try,
Is there a way?

For me to be strong,
I am crying all alone, scared all alone,
My life in the hell,
Daddy doesn't like me.

Mummy doesn't say much – nothing at all,
I am always beaten, never treated well,
Bruises on my face, thrashes on my back,

Makes it clear.

Church Bell Chimes

Today is a day I will always remember,
To start of the day as just two people in love,
And end it as husband and wife, the greatest in anyone's life.
It is a brand-new beginning, the start of a journey.

Though there be times when we both disagree,
Will sure be outweighed by pleasure,
I have heard many words of advice in the past,
When the secrets of marriage were spoken.

Now I know that the answers lie hidden inside,
To live happy forever as lovers and friends,
Dawn of a new life for us, as we stand there together,
With love in your eyes from the moment you whisper, "I do."

And with luck, all our hopes and our dreams can be real,
May success find its way to our hearts?
Tomorrow can bring us the greatest of joys,
Today is the day it all starts.

Two hands to hold on to forever,
Two arms to be embraced by eternally,
Two eyes to gaze into for always,
Two lips to kiss so passionately.

Two souls fused by commitment,
Two names written in the stars above,
Two lives intertwined by God,
Two hearts joined by the purest love.

Vows to take, and prayers to say,
On our blessed wedding day,
The dream has been seen, and whims thought,
And the angels dress already bought.

My little girl fantasy will come to life,
When we come together as man and wife.
The day church be filled with stars,
Coming from the gatherings, both near and far.

I cannot promise you a life of sunshine,
I cannot promise riches, wealth, or gold,
I cannot promise you an easy pathway,
Leads away from change or growing old.

I can promise all my heart's piety,
A smile to chase away your tears of sorrow,
A love that is ever true and growing,
A hand to hold in yours through each tomorrow.

The wedding bells will ring and choirs start to sing,
And down the aisle I'll walk to see you with,
My wedding ring with so much love and happiness,
In my heart we will no more be apart.

All our dreams about to come true,
I will be perfect wife and you will be the husband,
Tears will shed when exchanging the rings,
I will look lovely before him in a snowy white,

An angel is such a wondrous sight,
Filled with joy and love, blessing from up above,
Sadly, the day must come to an end,
The angel has now a lover and friend.

From this day forward,
You shall not walk alone,
My heart will be your shelter,
And my arms will be your home.

Living together cherishing every moment,
Loving each other as husband and wife,
Taking trips, seeing sights,
With disagreement but together by pleasure.

Vigilant with Tears

I pretend that I am sitting in a park, in the shadow of Notre
Dame, maybe it's going to rain, a cool breeze, and a gargoyle
from the cathedral looks down on me. How can a beast speak?
With a stone tongue and stone throat?

Standing in the warmth and looking out,
On the dark shadows illuminated for the moment,
By the break in my eyes,
As they are pushed aside frame by frame.

The moon light is on, concealed by the side of cathedral,
Yet in its warm, soft glow, I see my gargoyle,
And in that moment, the rain dripping down its face,
Take on a different look.

The glazing of tears, flowing down its cheeks,
And my gargoyle sits, heroic in all its glory,
Yet in that private moment, in that rainy day,
Shedding its tears, gargoyle tears!

He serves in humble obscurity,
High above the throngs who rarely see him
As they are too busy to look up,
And they don't like what he looks like.

None of whom has the power to save,
All of whom he prays will come to roost higher;
Sits, then upon the parapets of truth and reflects;
Does his best to guard good from evil, waits, thinks, and
watches.

The fairest of the gargoyles,
Was a beautiful hero, with wings,
And with a cape, and a face;
That was a mask all by itself.

He could have been a rainspout,
Pouring water fallen from the roof,
Of heaven, to roof of the building,
And on top of your head!

They draw my eyes and I observe,
With outstretched to scare the evil spirits,
Or are they talking, sad lives and their pain?
So, unlike mine but tangible to me, I pity the lot of you.

The gnarled and eerie features of stony face,
Worn by time, silent us in this cold lonely place,
What ancient craftsman shaped this?
Angel wings and mould its face unkind.

Thy spiteful muse did whisper maker's hand,
To hateful brow, to leering grin and evil crouching stand,
Eyes that only seem to glare, in anger at the fate,
That gave it only ugliness, made it to sit and wait.

I watch and wait, blink not till eyes are watery,
Moon fades and slowly grows morning,
Black birds have spoken and sun comes out,
And I am still sitting and waiting.

The Light House

The light house, the guardian angel of the night,
She shines her light for all the lost sailors passing by,
Her beam bright as the Sun, flashing through the night sky.

The light house, a soldier during the storms,
Standing tall, unafraid of the chaos
Her light piercing through the storm like sharp knives.

The light house the night owl of the day,
Sleeping and dozed away until the night,
Her beam off as silent as deer not wanting to be found.

But my mind goes back to one stormy night,
When just in time, I saw the light,
It was the light, from that old house, there upon the hill.

I thank the spirit for the light house,
I owe my life to Him, He is the light house,
Light around me, I clearly see. If it was not, where this ship be?

Flaming Forest

Down the road, across the highway street,
I have a busy home, I am a Gulmohar tree;
Each year from April to June, I am in full bloom,
Paint the streets with hues of red and orange.

Gentle summer breeze whisking through leaves
Burning and scarlet in the summer air,
Those pretty flowers, I gaze,
Petals appear like intense flames,
Dancing in the air like graceful dames.

What can rival the lovely hue,
Lining the roads across, glorious, colourful to see,
Made me hold my breath a while, desperate wish arises,
Wish to be here always, cut me not till I grow old.

Darn emotions on my petals, of flowers red,
Leaves turn sunny gold, I let them fall,
Those leaving, twirl down to ground;
Find a place of muddy ground of Earth.
Never regret being a Gulmohar tree.

Moods

Many emotions run deep within,
Head feels unclear, what to do,
Need to calm my emotions flowing through,
To feel grounded to Earth

An unlike mood and a changed way,
Sadness, anger, joy, grief, rage, loneliness,
Gladness, defeat, and despair.
More than nine, guides human thoughts.

They come in waves, cannot slow the setting,
You can only choose to untangle and say goodbye,
There is strength in you, you haven't even begun to find.

Forever we remain ignorant to the coming,
Lost to the past and enduring our pain.
We take chances to settle our scores,
Behind some fights and winning some battles.

I wish with all my might, could set things right,
In the world's broad field of battle,
With a heart for any fate, realising and chasing,
Learning to labour and pause.

Shopping Mall

I am at the mall shopping, a Saturday ritual,
Surrounded by people, couldn't find a trolley,
Hunted around, at last with the one with wonky wheel,

Walked into the busy packed shopping mall,
Some with smiles and others with frowns,
Added some are tired to go, shared a bench.

Hearing people, busy with their own thing;
Uncertain about their choices, some looking at their pockets;
Some looking for lockets, not sure which to choose.

Shoppers departing loaded down with thick carryalls,
The mall is of infinite things, so does the humans around,
I strode down the automobiles, through the streets to our silent
home.

Choices of Life

I smelled the sweet air,
Deeply and long, pure as prayer,
As sweet as song and roses wreath,
Heart – joy is I know just to breathe.

From mountain stream to covert cool,
The world I dream is wonderful,
The great, the small, the smooth, the rough,
I love it all, the smell or the breath is enough.

Our moments are precious, and time is now,
There is nothing to connect past and future,
The present only lasts but less than a breath,
So fast, a blink of an eye, it is the past.

It's been long since we built upon falsified memories;
Tonight, world will sleep, but life will go on,
We are all running through a bitter mind,
Curiosity, the only thing, makes life worth living.

It's been such a long time,
Since we last closed our eyes,
As fun is to laugh,
Is it not little better to live?

Cascade

Wandering aimlessly in the radiant ocean blue sky
Numerous decorated clouds, the day was blameless and sunlit.
The trees twirling like ballerinas, sending leaves on the way,
Waving their twigs like saluting people walking past

Threatening of a descending storm,
Dark clouds stretched across the horizon, devours the daylight,
The winds were fierce, screaming at us gnawing and clawing at
our home
Then came rain beating down upon us, thrown from the
darkened sky.

Banded by the howling of immense hurricane-like storm,
The rain gradually eased until finally fading into a charming
melody,
Like the graceful chimes of bells.
The gold rays peaked out, from behind a peaceful sheet of mist.

Casting slanted beams of light shining across the glass windows
Fluttering of wings could be heard as birds erupted from their
shelters
Trailed by a timely elegant song, feathered,
Amusingly over the building in harmony.

Hatching (New Life)

When evening came and the warm glow grew deeper,
A pigeon and his mate took their pleasure
Cuddling and hugging each other, like they have found a
paradise,
To paint an absolute love, without any fretful danger
Swirling and poising idly in golden light.
It has laid the promise of flight, float, and land,
With able skill, feverishly mate, to fast-flapping.
Feathers, curve an avian circle so effortless and so strong.
The dad treasures twigs to shape a nest
Mom lays one egg and takes off, incomes to a second one.
I'd go out on the balcony on while and watch them.
They'd stare back wide-eyed and freeze,
Her two tiny eggs fragile looking lightly streaked and white
Such a thing of natural beauty that only in nature is seen
Evolution lasts long days of twenty, Mom and Dad eagerly
await.
Squab remains in nest, outside my balcony
I can hear you in my room as you merrily serenade me
Your chirping is the sweetest my ears ever heard.

Gracefully

Grey hair a crown of glory, added in a good life,
Spread to the elderly in our life.
Rise and make them sense dear and loved
Our grandparents, aunts, uncles, or an elderly,
Style them feel special, a small sign means the most,
The beloved old friends in the family or society.
Heed to them not, as they are always right,
They have more wrong follows than us.
Never frown upon old age not for the law but of love.
Old age seen with distaste, stillness, and failure to work.
Elderly loved ones might be slowing down with age,
Never mean they don't want to celebrate.
Ways to train the cultures, to lifestyle for celebrations.
Spent at snaps together, delight their favourite music,
Walk together, places likely they can walk,
Stories shared are true treasures,
Stronger by weakness, wiser men become
As they draw near to their eternal home.

Nocturnal Blooms

Crimson curtain falls, sun goes off to sleep
Bright moon enveloped in black;
Starts budding, all through the nigh the flowers flare,
Small pearls unfold, white as a bridal gown
Blooms in beauty, fragrance calling the deepest senses,
The night is hers, drenched in dew
Pale moonlight caresses her skin,
Twinkling white flowers, alluring at night.
The day breaks, tree silently sheds
It's crowning glory, on mother earth.
Nothing changes; fragrance of jasmine,
Flaps and drifts, living for itself.

Spring

Bellowing winter bows away;
Spring is here and the sun is bright,
Nothing is so beautiful as spring
Fresh spring fragrance floating on the breeze,
Stirring the world from its frozen sleep.
Pretty flowers sing, green leaves dancing in air,
Trees are coming into leaf and flowers come to life
Blossoms on roads and fields, buds relax and spread
Time for renewal, out of hibernation;
Begins afresh from snow covered
Somewhere a deer has risen from sleep,
As the flowers beside dance and fly.
Sweet scents tickle your nose.
Myriad colours paint their blooms,
Dazzling beauty please our eyes.

Rain

The bright blue sky
Goes pale in confusion;
Clouded skies unite and demonise;
Just another rainy day.

The dusty plight of days of brutal,
Beating sun and sweltering heat.
Splashes on the footpath,
Dribbles down the drain.

Soaks all the garden,
Washes every tree.
Drifting off in slumber deep
Patiently I await your return.

The smell of sweet fresh rain.
Makes everything beautiful,
Loves walking in the rain
or even playing in puddles;
Wash away the pain of yesterday,
Listening to the rhythm of falling rain.

Jealousy

An emotion so wildly strong
Anger and jealousy are siblings
We are all told to be careful,
It's been known to break hearts

Slow poison stealing the peace of mind
Own over your innocent heart,
A silent rage that flows, burns inside
Changing you around, hurt inside.

Monstrous crawls up my back
Worms it to my brain
Thoughts are no longer mine
A sign of insecurity, weakness, obsession.

From the seed you unknowingly sow
You see it coming, feeding thoughts;
Tweak it off, can you? Before gaining grounds,
Trust me, when I tell you LOVE.

Rituals

A form of self-care, a promise,
A candle lit, prayers spoken, dip in river, crows fed;
Rituals are vital, comforts the soul, revive the spirit
Connects our past, present, and future selves,
Inward is protected and set apart from the world.
Something that stays, affords a sense of comfort and love.
Best rituals are reflex, speak so deeply to us, they just happen.
But any ritual can be shaped, it can be created.
Repeated actions have a sense of the religious to them,
Something that we carry with us as time passes.
A form of self-love, or comfort as we continue
The relationship, we have with ourselves.
Rituals are one way to discover and maintain inner truth.
Formulas by which harmony is restored, passage of soul into
infinite.

Family

A soft and gentle word, yet so strong,
If broken or destroyed, can be woven again.
Much like a book tells a specific relative's story
With the family name embossed on the cover forever
Tales bind us and tell the story of our family
Pass the book on, so coming generations will know.
A foundation to stand, when things go wrong,
A place built through years, of tiffs and tears,
Of laughter, joy and of love, know you deep inside,
Who'll pick you up each time you fall,
With love, from memories of when you were small,
The people who know your worst and your best
They're the loved ones with whom you're hallowed.
Near or far apart, that love will hold you close.

Growing Old

One day, looking in that mirror
I see a stranger there, looking back
Wonder where she is seen somewhere
I see me, don't you see, could it be me?

Things that meant the most are no longer in life.
People most important missing now from sight.
Too often my memory fails me, one minute I know
what I plan to do, and the next it may just slip my mind.

Deep in my hidden heart;
Festers the dull remembrance of a change,
Silvery hair and shrunken cheeks,
On eyes a pair of specs antique.

Missing

I was broken, simply need self-care and healing
I was unlovable, seeking love from gifted sources
I was unwanted, need self-confidence for better me
Thought was ugly, need appreciating my uniqueness.

I was uncertain and struggling, a period of growth and
evolution
When I thought I was lazy I was at period of rest
I was at lost, but was finding my new way
Thought was a failure, but my focus was shifting.

Never at lost that cannot be found and broken cannot be fixed
Never so wounded that cannot be loved, so sad and again feel
happy
Never so heartbroken so cannot find hope, so confused to find
clarity
Never too old to dream anew, all lonely designed to be loved.

There comes peace for all chaos, darkness removed and lit your
shadows
Let calmness come in the angry you, release the heavy burdens
Let there be healing, compassion heals your imperfectness
Let there come an abundance of love to all that is lonely.

Fate

Deep in me sits my fast fate, hope has sold me
Fallen in grief's furnace and suddenly burned
Followed me in unforeseen absolute road
High on expectation I might have been overdosed
Fate following us behind fastens it and we stop no more
Oh! Fate you were tissue of silver, wear grey;
Beamingly vague and radiant, dressed like moon.
The soul faces fate with daily will, defeated still
Gather strength returning like waves,
My heart with great despair, with my people's care
I mark faith's fragile skills of cheering light
Spirit shall rule and fate will obey
Endow a moment with my mood
High on expectation I might have overdosed.

Emotions

Anguish is love searching for a place to go
Sadness is idle talent, yearning to be expressed
Envy, a mirror, reveals to us what we desire
Shame, a recognition of past mistake and a desire to be better
Heartbreak, we have hyped another person's opinion of us,
Trusting how they see us is livelier than how we see
Resentment, an echo that we are not placing ourselves
And fear, is purely a sign that we are fully alive;
And are daring to step outside of our comfort zones
Learn what it means to truly live.
I owe myself an apology for all the times
Tore myself apart neglected my own needs
Let me the courage to change what I am gifted of;
The beauty to accept what is beyond my control
And choose my battles wisely to start anew.
Those who tried to dim my light taught me to shine wholly
Who chose to abandon me skilled me to never abandon myself
Those trials to silence me helped me to find my own voice
Thank you for teaching me to believe in myself.

Sundown

Something is truly magical as sky speaks in a thousand colours
As the sun lays down, and day stretches into sunset;
Meeting the distant horizon, never fails to take my breath away
I am in awe of its beauty, best is yet to come
Clouds veil the sunset, beauty hidden modestly,
That glowing orb of yellow sky, river sleeps beneath
Darkening from yellow to orange glow
I have never seen a sunset and not fall in love with,
It takes me to a place of serenity and confidence,
Sure, that life always renews with ending and beginnings.

Seasons

Autumn, has different coloured hair cascading down,
Favourite colours are orange, yellow, red, and sometimes green
People love her and place her in heart even if she is not around.
Spring is so lovely and kind, cares for birds and flowers perfect
in every way
Flowers adorn the head, hair so wavy and so brown cheery and
barely frowns;
Summer loved the beach, hot air blew through her hair, warm
heart
Tall and blonde with blue eyes, bright and happy drapes in
yellow,
Winter, blunt and harsh at times, cold and unforgiving, dark,
and distant
With cold white hair moon and sky danced with her wearing
oversized jackets,
Monsoon always cry and sometimes scream too, when she cries
looks like night;
Some are happy, sad and curse her, some ignores, ashamed and
embarrassed;
She would cry again and make her surrounds beautiful.

Clouds in Blue Sky

The clouds are blowing in, sun slowly disappears
Or is he playing hide and seek?
the white shape silhouetted
Against a blue background.
My favourite things,
Like to stare at clouds.

It changes every page
It is cotton cuddly
Cute and soft
Puffy and dark
Swiftly in the sky
Those puffy cumulus clouds
Are no sign of rain
But fair good weather.

They come in shapes,
Is it a rabbit, a dragon, a lion, or an angel?
Clouds are special for people and sun
Lots of different type
Black, grey, and white
Some fluffy and some flat.
Blocks the shiny sun
Birds and airplanes fly through
I like the cumulonimbus white clouds.

Dewdrops

Gleaming like a pearl drop to leaf blade
You are to the leaf a magic crystal
Dangling on necklet adds beauty to the leaf
Start twirling on the edge with all the skills
Light passes through creates a beautiful rainbow
If only you can hang on forever, can bear the sunlight
Each shiny dewdrop falls softly, onto the newly dampened
earth
To remind mortals nothing is forever, all returns to the giver
Loving does not always mean possessing,
Such is the morning dewdrop; you will forever be my delight.

Attic

I reach by climbing, steep narrow steps
The attic of an old country house
The room is small and low,
With slanting windows,
A row of skylights that leak rain,
And chatter in the winds.
I sleep beneath the roof's steep pitch,
My mattress flat on the boards,
Through the attic windows
Miracle of night sky amazed;
Lying on a hand-made comforter, protected
Against the cold night of stars.
Deep in the attic of my heart,
A chest is there that longs to be opened.
What is inside? Only I know,
Images and hums I claim I've forgotten.
Scrap-booked heaps of my life-tales;
Age has stolen so many.

Boundaries

Stretch for the boundaries is how we can grow
Starts with letting go to know your inner beauty
So much to reach out for, what is it you'll dream of
It's about breaking barriers, clearing confusion in the way
Healthy boundaries that support emotional being and time
Show love and respect for one, dream with all your heart
Pushing at the boundaries is where your future starts
With no boundaries blissful possibilities splash success!
Wings to experience the choice of flight to soar skies
Wisdom provides the boundaries that hold the chances we
create.

Myself

She will write you into her story
With a typewriter in her brain
She has a book shelf for a heart
With all the stories that she has penned
Ink runs through her veins
Her bookshelf getting crowded
Stories of every person she has met
Some has only one sentence, others hold main part;
Some she does not close, other she scared to open
One's who lost trust and sits collecting dust.
Thousands of inky footprints left her heart
She is quite in large groups, real me if we are close
Enjoy being alone, but outgoing and social
Situations dictates how she behaves
Awkward, clumsy, shy, strange, but this is me
Take it or leave it, hopes someone write about her too!

Grey Hair

Amid black tresses there gleamed a silvery thread
O silvery strand, thou soft kiss of time,
Pages of life, past and present I wonderingly then read.
Upon the shadowy dawn the small grey strand did lay
The mystic porches of life near ending stream
Beauties of youth are now past,
Evening of life are pleasures unknown,
Too often my memory fails me,
And my energy is not the same.
Things I used to do with ease
Now gives aches and pains
One minute I plan what to do,
Next minute it just slips my mind,
Underneath my worn-out shell,
I am still the same old me.
Still feel endless love, still can ache,
My heart fills with so much joy, then it suddenly breaks.
I am more willing to forgive, let past conflicts go.

Time

Bright and yellow, hard and cold
Stolen, borrowed, squandered,
Spurned by young but hung by old
Good or bad a thousand-fold!

To save, to ruin, to curse, to bless
New made friends like new wine;
Age will mellow and refine.
Torn pages of life flutter deep in golden abyss

Those pages crackling, prickling
Simple to ruin than harder to make life;
Reasons seems as the building chance
Time sipping through my hands.

Clock clicks and continues to chime
Moving through on nimble feet, forward and constant
Slowly ticks away, dust to dust I shall end my days
Brightly slanting for that trembling pause.

Bows an obedient head, hastes to bed
Drops the last courtesies,
Moments freeze, as to take a photo;
Capturing memory, we are time, lives in us…

www.ingramcontent.com/pod-product-compliance
Lightning Source LLC
Chambersburg PA
CBHW020509160726
47991CB00007B/2874